Nick Butte
Making Books

Written and illustrated by
Nick Butterworth

Collins

Hello! My name is Nick Butterworth.
I'm an author and an illustrator.

I write stories and draw pictures for
children's books.

Here are some of my books.

Here are some pictures of me when I was growing up.

This is me aged 13!

This is me!

4

My mum read us good stories.
I liked one called *Getup Crusoe*.
It was sad, but it was funny too!

Then Woeful (who should have known better) said the most hurtful thing any one can say to a little woollen giraffe who has lost his spots in a Stream. He said, "Humph! *All* the best woollen Animals are *fast-coloured*. Only cheap flannel coats run!"
Getup gave Woeful one long, reproachful look. And then he trotted away.

One long, reproachful look.

GETUP CRUSOE

Written and illustrated by
IVY L. WALLACE

My wife is called Annette.
We have two children called Ben
and Amanda.

Amanda
and Ben
with Annette
↓

Ben and Amanda are grown up now.
They are two of our best friends!

Amanda
and Ben as
children

Amanda
and Ben
grown up!

7

People sometimes ask, "Where do you get the ideas for your stories?"

This is Percy the Park Keeper

I got the idea for Percy the Park Keeper one day when I was in the park with our dog.

Percy the Park Keeper is like my
old grandpa. He was
a lovely man.

My grandpa
with my mum
and my brother

This picture of Percy makes me think of my grandpa in his shed.

I don't know how I got the idea for
Q Pootle 5. I was doodling one day
and he just seemed to pop out of
my pencil!

13

I love to draw animals.
All sorts of animals –

happy ones...

sad ones ...

funny ones.

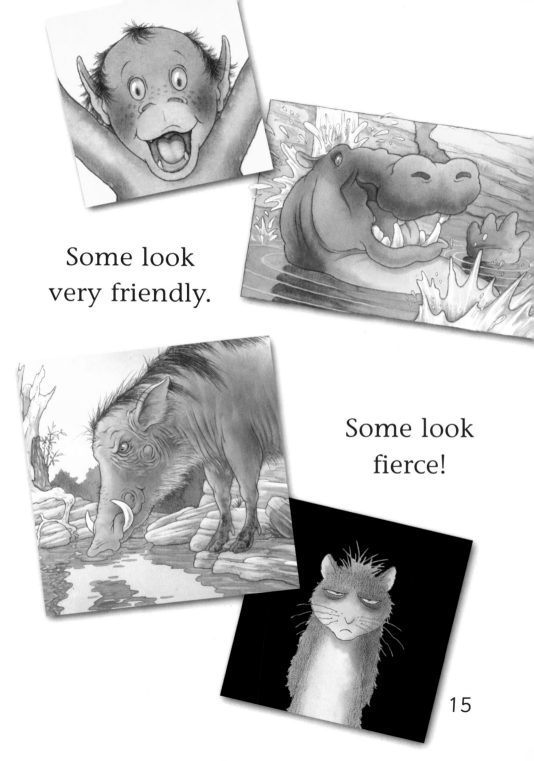

Some look
very friendly.

Some look
fierce!

I like to meet children when I go into schools.
It's fun to play drawing games and talk about my work.

Sometimes, children send letters
and pictures to me.

I work at home.
I have a special room
and a big desk where
I do my writing and
drawing.
It's hard work.
The pictures take a
long time to do.

When my stories and pictures are finished, I take them to a publisher.

The publisher makes them into books and puts them in shops.

It's nice to meet children in bookshops, too!

Three stages of drawing Percy the Park Keeper

1

2

3

Ideas for guided reading

Learning objectives: Use terms *fiction* and *non-fiction*, noting some of the differing features, e.g. layout, titles, contents page, use of pictures, labelled diagrams; read familiar texts aloud with pace and expression appropriate to the grammar; read on sight high frequency words.

Curriculum links: Art and design: building shapes and patterns; an issue/event in pictorial form

High frequency words: name, an, here, some, when, good, one, called, but, have, two, now, our, where, do, your, got, with, old, man, makes, his, don't, how, just, out, love, very, schools, about, home, take, time, them, puts, too

Interest words: Nick Butterworth, author, illustrator, Percy the Park Keeper, doodling, friendly, fierce, writing, publisher, bookshops

Word count: 311

Resources: books by Nick Butterworth, e.g. *Percy and the Badger* or *Percy and the Rabbit* (Collins Big Cat)

Getting started

- Cover the title and show the children the front cover. Ask them to guess what this person on the cover does for a job. Ensure that they can say and understand the words *author* and *illustrator*. Discuss who Nick Butterworth is (a leading children's author and illustrator).

- Read the blurb together. Ask the children to say what they think might give the author ideas for his books.

- Read pp2–3 to the children, pausing to discuss strategies to solve the words *author* and *illustrator*. Discuss the expression you used, particularly the informal tone suggested by 'Hello!'

- Ask the children to read pp2–3, encouraging them to read expressively. Then walk through the rest of the pages together, and ask them whether the book is fiction or non-fiction and to explain how they know (e.g. use of photographs, labels).